Runner's Weekly Log 2017 Complete Desk Diary

Copyright 2016

License Notes

2017

January

S	M	T	W	Th	F	S
1	2	3	4	5	6	7
8	9	10	11	12	13	14
15	16	17	18	19	20	21
22	23	24	25	26	27	28
29	30	31				

February

S	M	T	W	Th	F	S
			1	2	3	4
5	6	7	8	9	10	11
12	13	14	15	16	17	18
19	20	21	22	23	24	25
26	27	28				

March

S	M	T	W	Th	F	S
			1	2	3	4
5	6	7	8	9	10	11
12	13	14	15	16	17	18
19	20	21	22	23	24	25
26	27	28	29	30	31	

April

S	M	T	W	Th	F	S
						1
2	3	4	5	6	7	8
9	10	11	12	13	14	15
16	17	18	19	20	21	22
23	24	25	26	27	28	29
30						

May

S	M	T	W	Th	F	S
	1	2	3	4	5	6
7	8	9	10	11	12	13
14	15	16	17	18	19	20
21	22	23	24	25	26	27
28	29	30	31			

June

S	M	T	W	Th	F	S
				1	2	3
4	5	6	7	8	9	10
11	12	13	14	15	16	17
18	19	20	21	22	23	24
25	26	27	28	29	30	

July

S	M	T	W	Th	F	S
						1
2	3	4	5	6	7	8
9	10	11	12	13	14	15
16	17	18	19	20	21	22
23	24	25	26	27	28	29
30	31					

August

S	M	T	W	Th	F	S
		1	2	3	4	5
6	7	8	9	10	11	12
13	14	15	16	17	18	19
20	21	22	23	24	25	26
27	28	29	30	31		

September

S	M	T	W	Th	F	S
					1	2
3	4	5	6	7	8	9
10	11	12	13	14	15	16
17	18	19	20	21	22	23
24	25	26	27	28	29	30

October

S	M	T	W	Th	F	S
1	2	3	4	5	6	7
8	9	10	11	12	13	14
15	16	17	18	19	20	21
22	23	24	25	26	27	28
29	30	31				

November

S	M	T	W	Th	F	S
			1	2	3	4
5	6	7	8	9	10	11
12	13	14	15	16	17	18
19	20	21	22	23	24	25
26	27	28	29	30		

December

S	M	T	W	Th	F	S
					1	2
3	4	5	6	7	8	9
10	11	12	13	14	15	16
17	18	19	20	21	22	23
24	25	26	27	28	29	30
31						

PERSONAL DETAILS

NAME

ADDRESS

TELEPHONE NUMBER

COMPANY NAME/NUMBER

NHS NO

BLOOD GROUP

PASSPORT NO.

DRIVING LICENSE NO.

EMERGENCY NAME

EMERGENCY ADDRESS

EMERGENCY TEL NO:-

ATHLETICS 2017 IAAF Schedule & World Championships
IAAF Diamond League

MEETING	COUNTRY	DATE
Doha	QAT	05th May 2017
Shanghai	CHN	13th May 2017
Eugene	USA	27th May 2017
Rome	ITA	08th June 2017
Oslo	NOR	15th June 2017
Stockholm	SWE	18th June 2017
Paris	FRA	01st July 2017
Lausanne	SUI	06th July 2017
London	GBR	09th July 2017
Rabat	MAR	16th July 2017
Monaco	MON	21st July 2017

IAAF **WORLD CHAMPIONSHIPS** 4 - 13 AUG 2017 (London)

Birmingham	GBR	20th Aug 2017
Zurich	SUI	24th Aug 2017
Brussels	BEL	01st Sept 2017

Athletics World Record Times (Men)

Distance	Time	Athlete	Country	Date
100 m	9.58	Usain Bolt	Jamaica	19/08/09
200 m	19.19	Usain Bolt	Jamaica	16/08/09
400 m	43.03	Wayde van Niekerk	S.Africa	14/08/16
800 m	01:40.9	David Rudisha	Kenya	09/08/12
1000 m	02:12.0	Noah Ngeny	Kenya	05/09/99
1500 m	03:26.0	Hicham El Guerrouj	Morocco	14/07/98
Mile	03:43.1	Hicham El Guerrouj	Morocco	07/07/99
2000 m	04:44.8	Hicham El Guerrouj	Morocco	07/09/99
3000 m	07:20.7	Daniel Komen	Kenya	01/09/96
5000 m	12:37.4	Kenenisa Bekele	Ethiopia	31/05/04
10,000 m	26:17.5	Kenenisa Bekele	Ethiopia	26/08/05
10km (road)	26:44:00	Leonard Komon	Kenya	26/09/10
1/2 marathon	58:23:00	Zersenay Tadese	Eritrea	21/03/10
Marathon	02:02:57	Dennis Kimetto	Kenya	28/09/14

Athletics World Record Times (Women)

Distance	Time	Athlete	Country	Date
100 m	10.49	Florence G Joyner	USA	16/07/88
200 m	21.34	Florence G Joyner	USA	29/09/88
400 m	47.6	Marita Koch	East Ger	06/10/85
800 m	01:53.3	Jarmila Kratochvílová	Czech	26/07/83
1000 m	02:29.0	Svetlana Masterkova	Russia	23/08/96
1500 m	03:50.0	Genzebe Dibaba	Ethiopia	17/07/15
Mile	04:12.6	Svetlana Masterkova	Russia	14/08/96
2000 m	05:25.4	Sonia O'Sullivan	Ireland	08/07/94
3000 m	08:06.1	Wang Junxia	China	13/09/93
5000 m	14:11.2	Tirunesh Dibaba	Ethiopia	06/06/08
10,000 m	29:17.4	Almaz Ayana	Ethiopia	12/08/16
10km (road)	30:21:00	Paula Radcliffe	GB	23/02/03
1/2 marathon	01:01:54	Florence Kiplagat	Kenya	15/02/15
Marathon	02:15:25	Paula Radcliffe	GB	13/04/03

Monday 26/12/2016 To Sunday 01/01/2017

			Daily Training						
Weather			**M**	**T**	**W**	**T**	**F**	**S**	**S**
(e.g.1) Slight headwind /cold	7	:00							
		:30							
	8	:00							
		:15							
		:30							
		:45							
	9	:00							
		:15							
		:30							
		:45	e.g.1						
	10	:00							
Running Distance		:15							
(e.g.1) Ingthorpe Route 1.48		:30							
- Turned right at park		:45							
	11	:00							
		:15							
		:30							
		:45							
	12	:00							
		:15							
		:30							
		:45							
	1	:00							
		:15							
		:30							
		:45							
	2	:00							
		:15							
		:30							
Time		:45							
(e.g.1) 16 min 50 s	3	:00							
		:15							
		:30							
		:45							
	4	:00							
		:15							
		:30							
		:45							
	5	:00							
Comments		:30							
(e.g.1) Totally shattered!!	6	:00							
		:30							
	7	:00							
		:30							
	8	:00							
		:30							

Monday 02/01/2017 To Sunday 08/01/2017

Weather			Daily Training						
			M	T	W	T	F	S	S
	7	:00							
		:30							
	8	:00							
		:15							
		:30							
		:45							
	9	:00							
		:15							
		:30							
		:45							
Running Distance	10	:00							
		:15							
		:30							
		:45							
	11	:00							
		:15							
		:30							
		:45							
	12	:00							
		:15							
		:30							
		:45							
	1	:00							
		:15							
		:30							
		:45							
	2	:00							
		:15							
		:30							
Time		:45							
	3	:00							
		:15							
		:30							
		:45							
	4	:00							
		:15							
		:30							
		:45							
	5	:00							
Comments		:30							
	6	:00							
		:30							
	7	:00							
		:30							
	8	:00							
		:30							

8

Daily Training

Weather			M	T	W	T	F	S	S
	7	:00							
		:30							
	8	:00							
		:15							
		:30							
		:45							
	9	:00							
		:15							
		:30							
		:45							
Running Distance	10	:00							
		:15							
		:30							
		:45							
	11	:00							
		:15							
		:30							
		:45							
	12	:00							
		:15							
		:30							
		:45							
	1	:00							
		:15							
		:30							
		:45							
	2	:00							
		:15							
		:30							
Time		:45							
	3	:00							
		:15							
		:30							
		:45							
	4	:00							
		:15							
		:30							
		:45							
	5	:00							
Comments		:30							
	6	:00							
		:30							
	7	:00							
		:30							
	8	:00							
		:30							

Monday 16/01/2017 To Sunday 22/01/2017

Weather				Daily Training					
			M	T	W	T	F	S	S
	7	:00							
		:30							
	8	:00							
		:15							
		:30							
		:45							
	9	:00							
		:15							
		:30							
		:45							
	10	:00							
Running Distance		:15							
		:30							
		:45							
	11	:00							
		:15							
		:30							
		:45							
	12	:00							
		:15							
		:30							
		:45							
	1	:00							
		:15							
		:30							
		:45							
	2	:00							
		:15							
		:30							
Time		:45							
	3	:00							
		:15							
		:30							
		:45							
	4	:00							
		:15							
		:30							
		:45							
	5	:00							
Comments		:30							
	6	:00							
		:30							
	7	:00							
		:30							
	8	:00							
		:30							

Monday 23/01/2017 To Sunday 29/01/2017

Weather			Daily Training						
			M	T	W	T	F	S	S
	7	:00							
		:30							
	8	:00							
		:15							
		:30							
		:45							
	9	:00							
		:15							
		:30							
		:45							
	10	:00							
Running Distance		:15							
		:30							
		:45							
	11	:00							
		:15							
		:30							
		:45							
	12	:00							
		:15							
		:30							
		:45							
	1	:00							
		:15							
		:30							
		:45							
	2	:00							
		:15							
		:30							
Time		:45							
	3	:00							
		:15							
		:30							
		:45							
	4	:00							
		:15							
		:30							
		:45							
	5	:00							
Comments		:30							
	6	:00							
		:30							
	7	:00							
		:30							
	8	:00							
		:30							

Daily Training

Weather			M	T	W	T	F	S	S
	7	:00							
		:30							
	8	:00							
		:15							
		:30							
		:45							
	9	:00							
		:15							
		:30							
		:45							
	10	:00							
Running Distance		:15							
		:30							
		:45							
	11	:00							
		:15							
		:30							
		:45							
	12	:00							
		:15							
		:30							
		:45							
	1	:00							
		:15							
		:30							
		:45							
	2	:00							
		:15							
		:30							
Time		:45							
	3	:00							
		:15							
		:30							
		:45							
	4	:00							
		:15							
		:30							
		:45							
	5	:00							
Comments		:30							
	6	:00							
		:30							
	7	:00							
		:30							
	8	:00							
		:30							

Monday 06/02/2017 To Sunday 12/02/2017

Weather				Daily Training						
			M	T	W	T	F	S	S
	7	:00							
		:30							
	8	:00							
		:15							
		:30							
		:45							
	9	:00							
		:15							
		:30							
		:45							
Running Distance	10	:00							
		:15							
		:30							
		:45							
	11	:00							
		:15							
		:30							
		:45							
	12	:00							
		:15							
		:30							
		:45							
	1	:00							
		:15							
		:30							
		:45							
	2	:00							
		:15							
		:30							
Time		:45							
	3	:00							
		:15							
		:30							
		:45							
	4	:00							
		:15							
		:30							
		:45							
	5	:00							
Comments		:30							
	6	:00							
		:30							
	7	:00							
		:30							
	8	:00							
		:30							

Daily Training

Weather			M	T	W	T	F	S	S
	7	:00							
		:30							
	8	:00							
		:15							
		:30							
		:45							
	9	:00							
		:15							
		:30							
		:45							
Running Distance	10	:00							
		:15							
		:30							
		:45							
	11	:00							
		:15							
		:30							
		:45							
	12	:00							
		:15							
		:30							
		:45							
	1	:00							
		:15							
		:30							
		:45							
	2	:00							
		:15							
		:30							
Time		:45							
	3	:00							
		:15							
		:30							
		:45							
	4	:00							
		:15							
		:30							
		:45							
	5	:00							
Comments		:30							
	6	:00							
		:30							
	7	:00							
		:30							
	8	:00							
		:30							

14

Monday 20/02/2017 To Sunday 26/02/2017

Weather		Daily Training							
		M	T	W	T	F	S	S
	7 :00								
	:30								
	8 :00								
	:15								
	:30								
	:45								
	9 :00								
	:15								
	:30								
	:45								
Running Distance	10 :00								
	:15								
	:30								
	:45								
	11 :00								
	:15								
	:30								
	:45								
	12 :00								
	:15								
	:30								
	:45								
	1 :00								
	:15								
	:30								
	:45								
	2 :00								
	:15								
	:30								
Time	:45								
	3 :00								
	:15								
	:30								
	:45								
	4 :00								
	:15								
	:30								
	:45								
	5 :00								
Comments	:30								
	6 :00								
	:30								
	7 :00								
	:30								
	8 :00								
	:30								

Daily Training

Weather			M	T	W	T	F	S	S
	7	:00							
		:30							
	8	:00							
		:15							
		:30							
		:45							
	9	:00							
		:15							
		:30							
		:45							
	10	:00							
Running Distance		:15							
		:30							
		:45							
	11	:00							
		:15							
		:30							
		:45							
	12	:00							
		:15							
		:30							
		:45							
	1	:00							
		:15							
		:30							
		:45							
	2	:00							
		:15							
		:30							
Time		:45							
	3	:00							
		:15							
		:30							
		:45							
	4	:00							
		:15							
		:30							
		:45							
	5	:00							
Comments		:30							
	6	:00							
		:30							
	7	:00							
		:30							
	8	:00							
		:30							

Monday 06/03/2017 To Sunday 12/03/2017

Weather			Daily Training						
			M	T	W	T	F	S	S
	7	:00							
		:30							
	8	:00							
		:15							
		:30							
		:45							
	9	:00							
		:15							
		:30							
		:45							
Running Distance	10	:00							
		:15							
		:30							
		:45							
	11	:00							
		:15							
		:30							
		:45							
	12	:00							
		:15							
		:30							
		:45							
	1	:00							
		:15							
		:30							
		:45							
	2	:00							
		:15							
		:30							
Time		:45							
	3	:00							
		:15							
		:30							
		:45							
	4	:00							
		:15							
		:30							
		:45							
	5	:00							
Comments		:30							
	6	:00							
		:30							
	7	:00							
		:30							
	8	:00							
		:30							

Weather			M	T	W	T	F	S	S
	7	:00							
		:30							
	8	:00							
		:15							
		:30							
		:45							
	9	:00							
		:15							
		:30							
		:45							
Running Distance	10	:00							
		:15							
		:30							
		:45							
	11	:00							
		:15							
		:30							
		:45							
	12	:00							
		:15							
		:30							
		:45							
	1	:00							
		:15							
		:30							
		:45							
	2	:00							
		:15							
		:30							
Time		:45							
	3	:00							
		:15							
		:30							
		:45							
	4	:00							
		:15							
		:30							
		:45							
	5	:00							
Comments		:30							
	6	:00							
		:30							
	7	:00							
		:30							
	8	:00							
		:30							

Monday 20/03/2017 To Sunday 26/03/2017

Weather			Daily Training						
			M	T	W	T	F	S	S
	7 :00								
	:30								
	8 :00								
	:15								
	:30								
	:45								
	9 :00								
	:15								
	:30								
	:45								
Running Distance	10 :00								
	:15								
	:30								
	:45								
	11 :00								
	:15								
	:30								
	:45								
	12 :00								
	:15								
	:30								
	:45								
	1 :00								
	:15								
	:30								
	:45								
	2 :00								
	:15								
	:30								
Time	:45								
	3 :00								
	:15								
	:30								
	:45								
	4 :00								
	:15								
	:30								
	:45								
	5 :00								
Comments	:30								
	6 :00								
	:30								
	7 :00								
	:30								
	8 :00								
	:30								

19

Weather			M	T	W	T	F	S	S
	7	:00							
		:30							
	8	:00							
		:15							
		:30							
		:45							
	9	:00							
		:15							
		:30							
		:45							
	10	:00							
Running Distance		:15							
		:30							
		:45							
	11	:00							
		:15							
		:30							
		:45							
	12	:00							
		:15							
		:30							
		:45							
	1	:00							
		:15							
		:30							
		:45							
	2	:00							
		:15							
		:30							
Time		:45							
	3	:00							
		:15							
		:30							
		:45							
	4	:00							
		:15							
		:30							
		:45							
	5	:00							
Comments		:30							
	6	:00							
		:30							
	7	:00							
		:30							
	8	:00							
		:30							

Monday 03/04/2017 To Sunday 09/04/2017

Weather			M	T	W	T	F	S	S
	7	:00							
		:30							
	8	:00							
		:15							
		:30							
		:45							
	9	:00							
		:15							
		:30							
		:45							
Running Distance	10	:00							
		:15							
		:30							
		:45							
	11	:00							
		:15							
		:30							
		:45							
	12	:00							
		:15							
		:30							
		:45							
	1	:00							
		:15							
		:30							
		:45							
	2	:00							
		:15							
		:30							
Time		:45							
	3	:00							
		:15							
		:30							
		:45							
	4	:00							
		:15							
		:30							
		:45							
	5	:00							
Comments		:30							
	6	:00							
		:30							
	7	:00							
		:30							
	8	:00							
		:30							

Monday 10/04/2017 To Sunday 16/04/2017

Weather			Daily Training						
			M	T	W	T	F	S	S
	7 :00								
	:30								
	8 :00								
	:15								
	:30								
	:45								
	9 :00								
	:15								
	:30								
	:45								
Running Distance	10 :00								
	:15								
	:30								
	:45								
	11 :00								
	:15								
	:30								
	:45								
	12 :00								
	:15								
	:30								
	:45								
	1 :00								
	:15								
	:30								
	:45								
	2 :00								
	:15								
	:30								
Time	:45								
	3 :00								
	:15								
	:30								
	:45								
	4 :00								
	:15								
	:30								
	:45								
	5 :00								
Comments	:30								
	6 :00								
	:30								
	7 :00								
	:30								
	8 :00								
	:30								

Monday 17/04/2017 To Sunday 23/04/2017

Weather			Daily Training							
			M	T	W	T	F	S	S
	7	:00							
		:30							
	8	:00							
		:15							
		:30							
		:45							
	9	:00							
		:15							
		:30							
		:45							
Running Distance	10	:00							
		:15							
		:30							
		:45							
	11	:00							
		:15							
		:30							
		:45							
	12	:00							
		:15							
		:30							
		:45							
	1	:00							
		:15							
		:30							
		:45							
	2	:00							
		:15							
		:30							
Time		:45							
	3	:00							
		:15							
		:30							
		:45							
	4	:00							
		:15							
		:30							
		:45							
	5	:00							
Comments		:30							
	6	:00							
		:30							
	7	:00							
		:30							
	8	:00							
		:30							

Monday 24/04/2017 To Sunday 30/04/2017

Weather			Daily Training						
			M	T	W	T	F	S	S
	7	:00							
		:30							
	8	:00							
		:15							
		:30							
		:45							
	9	:00							
		:15							
		:30							
		:45							
	10	:00							
Running Distance		:15							
		:30							
		:45							
	11	:00							
		:15							
		:30							
		:45							
	12	:00							
		:15							
		:30							
		:45							
	1	:00							
		:15							
		:30							
		:45							
	2	:00							
		:15							
		:30							
Time		:45							
	3	:00							
		:15							
		:30							
		:45							
	4	:00							
		:15							
		:30							
		:45							
	5	:00							
Comments		:30							
	6	:00							
		:30							
	7	:00							
		:30							
	8	:00							
		:30							

Monday 01/05/2017 To Sunday 07/05/2017

				Daily Training					
Weather				M	T	W	T	F	S	S

Weather			M	T	W	T	F	S	S
	7	:00							
		:30							
	8	:00							
		:15							
		:30							
		:45							
	9	:00							
		:15							
		:30							
		:45							
Running Distance	10	:00							
		:15							
		:30							
		:45							
	11	:00							
		:15							
		:30							
		:45							
	12	:00							
		:15							
		:30							
		:45							
	1	:00							
		:15							
		:30							
		:45							
	2	:00							
		:15							
		:30							
Time		:45							
	3	:00							
		:15							
		:30							
		:45							
	4	:00							
		:15							
		:30							
		:45							
	5	:00							
Comments		:30							
	6	:00							
		:30							
	7	:00							
		:30							
	8	:00							
		:30							

						Daily Training				
Weather			**M**	**T**	**W**	**T**	**F**	**S**	**S**
	7	:00							
		:30							
	8	:00							
		:15							
		:30							
		:45							
	9	:00							
		:15							
		:30							
		:45							
Running Distance	10	:00							
		:15							
		:30							
		:45							
	11	:00							
		:15							
		:30							
		:45							
	12	:00							
		:15							
		:30							
		:45							
	1	:00							
		:15							
		:30							
		:45							
	2	:00							
		:15							
		:30							
Time		:45							
	3	:00							
		:15							
		:30							
		:45							
	4	:00							
		:15							
		:30							
		:45							
	5	:00							
Comments		:30							
	6	:00							
		:30							
	7	:00							
		:30							
	8	:00							
		:30							

Monday 15/05/2017 To Sunday 21/05/2017

Weather			Daily Training							
			M	T	W	T	F	S	S
	7	:00							
		:30							
	8	:00							
		:15							
		:30							
		:45							
	9	:00							
		:15							
		:30							
		:45							
Running Distance	10	:00							
		:15							
		:30							
		:45							
	11	:00							
		:15							
		:30							
		:45							
	12	:00							
		:15							
		:30							
		:45							
	1	:00							
		:15							
		:30							
		:45							
	2	:00							
		:15							
		:30							
Time		:45							
	3	:00							
		:15							
		:30							
		:45							
	4	:00							
		:15							
		:30							
		:45							
	5	:00							
Comments		:30							
	6	:00							
		:30							
	7	:00							
		:30							
	8	:00							
		:30							

Monday 22/05/2017 To Sunday 28/05/2017

Weather					Daily Training					
			M	T	W	T	F	S	S
	7	:00							
		:30							
	8	:00							
		:15							
		:30							
		:45							
	9	:00							
		:15							
		:30							
		:45							
Running Distance	10	:00							
		:15							
		:30							
		:45							
	11	:00							
		:15							
		:30							
		:45							
	12	:00							
		:15							
		:30							
		:45							
	1	:00							
		:15							
		:30							
		:45							
	2	:00							
		:15							
		:30							
Time		:45							
	3	:00							
		:15							
		:30							
		:45							
	4	:00							
		:15							
		:30							
		:45							
	5	:00							
Comments		:30							
	6	:00							
		:30							
	7	:00							
		:30							
	8	:00							
		:30							

Weather		Daily Training						
		M	T	W	T	F	S	S
	7 :00							
	:30							
	8 :00							
	:15							
	:30							
	:45							
	9 :00							
	:15							
	:30							
	:45							
Running Distance	10 :00							
	:15							
	:30							
	:45							
	11 :00							
	:15							
	:30							
	:45							
	12 :00							
	:15							
	:30							
	:45							
	1 :00							
	:15							
	:30							
	:45							
	2 :00							
	:15							
	:30							
Time	:45							
	3 :00							
	:15							
	:30							
	:45							
	4 :00							
	:15							
	:30							
	:45							
	5 :00							
Comments	:30							
	6 :00							
	:30							
	7 :00							
	:30							
	8 :00							
	:30							

Monday 05/06/2017 To Sunday 11/06/2017

Weather			Daily Training							
			M	T	W	T	F	S	S
	7	:00							
		:30							
	8	:00							
		:15							
		:30							
		:45							
	9	:00							
		:15							
		:30							
		:45							
	10	:00							
Running Distance		:15							
		:30							
		:45							
	11	:00							
		:15							
		:30							
		:45							
	12	:00							
		:15							
		:30							
		:45							
	1	:00							
		:15							
		:30							
		:45							
	2	:00							
		:15							
		:30							
Time		:45							
	3	:00							
		:15							
		:30							
		:45							
	4	:00							
		:15							
		:30							
		:45							
	5	:00							
Comments		:30							
	6	:00							
		:30							
	7	:00							
		:30							
	8	:00							
		:30							

Weather			Daily Training							
			M	T	W	T	F	S	S
	7	:00							
		:30							
	8	:00							
		:15							
		:30							
		:45							
	9	:00							
		:15							
		:30							
		:45							
Running Distance	10	:00							
		:15							
		:30							
		:45							
	11	:00							
		:15							
		:30							
		:45							
	12	:00							
		:15							
		:30							
		:45							
	1	:00							
		:15							
		:30							
		:45							
	2	:00							
		:15							
		:30							
Time		:45							
	3	:00							
		:15							
		:30							
		:45							
	4	:00							
		:15							
		:30							
		:45							
	5	:00							
Comments		:30							
	6	:00							
		:30							
	7	:00							
		:30							
	8	:00							
		:30							

Monday 19/06/2017 To Sunday 25/06/2017

Weather			M	T	W	T	F	S	S
	7	:00							
		:30							
	8	:00							
		:15							
		:30							
		:45							
	9	:00							
		:15							
		:30							
		:45							
Running Distance	10	:00							
		:15							
		:30							
		:45							
	11	:00							
		:15							
		:30							
		:45							
	12	:00							
		:15							
		:30							
		:45							
	1	:00							
		:15							
		:30							
		:45							
	2	:00							
		:15							
		:30							
Time		:45							
	3	:00							
		:15							
		:30							
		:45							
	4	:00							
		:15							
		:30							
		:45							
	5	:00							
Comments		:30							
	6	:00							
		:30							
	7	:00							
		:30							
	8	:00							
		:30							

Daily Training

Monday 26/06/2017 To Sunday 02/07/2017

				Daily Training					
Weather			M	T	W	T	F	S	S
	7	:00							
		:30							
	8	:00							
		:15							
		:30							
		:45							
	9	:00							
		:15							
		:30							
		:45							
Running Distance	10	:00							
		:15							
		:30							
		:45							
	11	:00							
		:15							
		:30							
		:45							
	12	:00							
		:15							
		:30							
		:45							
	1	:00							
		:15							
		:30							
		:45							
	2	:00							
		:15							
		:30							
Time		:45							
	3	:00							
		:15							
		:30							
		:45							
	4	:00							
		:15							
		:30							
		:45							
	5	:00							
Comments		:30							
	6	:00							
		:30							
	7	:00							
		:30							
	8	:00							
		:30							

			M	T	W	T	F	S	S
Weather		Daily Training							
	7	:00							
		:30							
	8	:00							
		:15							
		:30							
		:45							
	9	:00							
		:15							
		:30							
		:45							
	10	:00							
Running Distance		:15							
		:30							
		:45							
	11	:00							
		:15							
		:30							
		:45							
	12	:00							
		:15							
		:30							
		:45							
	1	:00							
		:15							
		:30							
		:45							
	2	:00							
		:15							
		:30							
Time		:45							
	3	:00							
		:15							
		:30							
		:45							
	4	:00							
		:15							
		:30							
		:45							
	5	:00							
Comments		:30							
	6	:00							
		:30							
	7	:00							
		:30							
	8	:00							
		:30							

Monday 10/07/2017 To Sunday 16/07/2017

					Daily Training			
Weather			M	T	W	T	F	S	S

Weather			M	T	W	T	F	S	S
	7	:00							
		:30							
	8	:00							
		:15							
		:30							
		:45							
	9	:00							
		:15							
		:30							
		:45							
Running Distance	10	:00							
		:15							
		:30							
		:45							
	11	:00							
		:15							
		:30							
		:45							
	12	:00							
		:15							
		:30							
		:45							
	1	:00							
		:15							
		:30							
		:45							
	2	:00							
		:15							
		:30							
Time		:45							
	3	:00							
		:15							
		:30							
		:45							
	4	:00							
		:15							
		:30							
		:45							
	5	:00							
Comments		:30							
	6	:00							
		:30							
	7	:00							
		:30							
	8	:00							
		:30							

Monday 17/07/2017 To Sunday 23/07/2017

					Daily Training			
Weather		**M**	**T**	**W**	**T**	**F**	**S**	**S**
	7 :00							
	:30							
	8 :00							
	:15							
	:30							
	:45							
	9 :00							
	:15							
	:30							
	:45							
Running Distance	10 :00							
	:15							
	:30							
	:45							
	11 :00							
	:15							
	:30							
	:45							
	12 :00							
	:15							
	:30							
	:45							
	1 :00							
	:15							
	:30							
	:45							
	2 :00							
	:15							
	:30							
Time	:45							
	3 :00							
	:15							
	:30							
	:45							
	4 :00							
	:15							
	:30							
	:45							
	5 :00							
Comments	:30							
	6 :00							
	:30							
	7 :00							
	:30							
	8 :00							
	:30							

Monday 24/07/2017 To Sunday 30/07/2017

Weather			Daily Training						
			M	T	W	T	F	S	S
	7	:00							
		:30							
	8	:00							
		:15							
		:30							
		:45							
	9	:00							
		:15							
		:30							
		:45							
	10	:00							
Running Distance		:15							
		:30							
		:45							
	11	:00							
		:15							
		:30							
		:45							
	12	:00							
		:15							
		:30							
		:45							
	1	:00							
		:15							
		:30							
		:45							
	2	:00							
		:15							
		:30							
Time		:45							
	3	:00							
		:15							
		:30							
		:45							
	4	:00							
		:15							
		:30							
		:45							
	5	:00							
Comments		:30							
	6	:00							
		:30							
	7	:00							
		:30							
	8	:00							
		:30							

Monday 31/07/2017 To Sunday 06/08/2017

Weather			Daily Training						
			M	T	W	T	F	S	S
	7	:00							
		:30							
	8	:00							
		:15							
		:30							
		:45							
	9	:00							
		:15							
		:30							
		:45							
Running Distance	10	:00							
		:15							
		:30							
		:45							
	11	:00							
		:15							
		:30							
		:45							
	12	:00							
		:15							
		:30							
		:45							
	1	:00							
		:15							
		:30							
		:45							
	2	:00							
		:15							
		:30							
Time		:45							
	3	:00							
		:15							
		:30							
		:45							
	4	:00							
		:15							
		:30							
		:45							
	5	:00							
Comments		:30							
	6	:00							
		:30							
	7	:00							
		:30							
	8	:00							
		:30							

Monday 07/08/2017 To Sunday 13/08/2017

Weather			M	T	W	T	F	S	S
	7	:00							
		:30							
	8	:00							
		:15							
		:30							
		:45							
	9	:00							
		:15							
		:30							
		:45							
Running Distance	10	:00							
		:15							
		:30							
		:45							
	11	:00							
		:15							
		:30							
		:45							
	12	:00							
		:15							
		:30							
		:45							
	1	:00							
		:15							
		:30							
		:45							
	2	:00							
		:15							
		:30							
Time		:45							
	3	:00							
		:15							
		:30							
		:45							
	4	:00							
		:15							
		:30							
		:45							
	5	:00							
Comments		:30							
	6	:00							
		:30							
	7	:00							
		:30							
	8	:00							
		:30							

Daily Training

Monday 14/08/2017 To Sunday 20/08/2017

Weather				Daily Training						
				M	T	W	T	F	S	S
	7	:00								
		:30								
	8	:00								
		:15								
		:30								
		:45								
	9	:00								
		:15								
		:30								
		:45								
	10	:00								
Running Distance		:15								
		:30								
		:45								
	11	:00								
		:15								
		:30								
		:45								
	12	:00								
		:15								
		:30								
		:45								
	1	:00								
		:15								
		:30								
		:45								
	2	:00								
		:15								
		:30								
Time		:45								
	3	:00								
		:15								
		:30								
		:45								
	4	:00								
		:15								
		:30								
		:45								
	5	:00								
Comments		:30								
	6	:00								
		:30								
	7	:00								
		:30								
	8	:00								
		:30								

Monday 21/08/2017 To Sunday 27/08/2017

Weather		Daily Training							
		M	T	W	T	F	S	S
	7 :00								
	:30								
	8 :00								
	:15								
	:30								
	:45								
	9 :00								
	:15								
	:30								
	:45								
Running Distance	10 :00								
	:15								
	:30								
	:45								
	11 :00								
	:15								
	:30								
	:45								
	12 :00								
	:15								
	:30								
	:45								
	1 :00								
	:15								
	:30								
	:45								
	2 :00								
	:15								
	:30								
Time	:45								
	3 :00								
	:15								
	:30								
	:45								
	4 :00								
	:15								
	:30								
	:45								
	5 :00								
Comments	:30								
	6 :00								
	:30								
	7 :00								
	:30								
	8 :00								
	:30								

Monday 28/08/2017 To Sunday 03/09/2017

Weather			M	T	W	T	F	S	S
	7	:00							
		:30							
	8	:00							
		:15							
		:30							
		:45							
	9	:00							
		:15							
		:30							
		:45							
Running Distance	10	:00							
		:15							
		:30							
		:45							
	11	:00							
		:15							
		:30							
		:45							
	12	:00							
		:15							
		:30							
		:45							
	1	:00							
		:15							
		:30							
		:45							
	2	:00							
		:15							
		:30							
Time		:45							
	3	:00							
		:15							
		:30							
		:45							
	4	:00							
		:15							
		:30							
		:45							
	5	:00							
Comments		:30							
	6	:00							
		:30							
	7	:00							
		:30							
	8	:00							
		:30							

Monday 04/09/2017 To Sunday 10/09/2017

Weather			Daily Training						
			M	T	W	T	F	S	S
	7	:00							
		:30							
	8	:00							
		:15							
		:30							
		:45							
	9	:00							
		:15							
		:30							
		:45							
	10	:00							
Running Distance		:15							
		:30							
		:45							
	11	:00							
		:15							
		:30							
		:45							
	12	:00							
		:15							
		:30							
		:45							
	1	:00							
		:15							
		:30							
		:45							
	2	:00							
		:15							
		:30							
Time		:45							
	3	:00							
		:15							
		:30							
		:45							
	4	:00							
		:15							
		:30							
		:45							
	5	:00							
Comments		:30							
	6	:00							
		:30							
	7	:00							
		:30							
	8	:00							
		:30							

Monday 11/09/2017 To Sunday 17/09/2017

			Daily Training						
Weather			M	T	W	T	F	S	S
	7	:00							
		:30							
	8	:00							
		:15							
		:30							
		:45							
	9	:00							
		:15							
		:30							
		:45							
	10	:00							
Running Distance		:15							
		:30							
		:45							
	11	:00							
		:15							
		:30							
		:45							
	12	:00							
		:15							
		:30							
		:45							
	1	:00							
		:15							
		:30							
		:45							
	2	:00							
		:15							
		:30							
Time		:45							
	3	:00							
		:15							
		:30							
		:45							
	4	:00							
		:15							
		:30							
		:45							
	5	:00							
Comments		:30							
	6	:00							
		:30							
	7	:00							
		:30							
	8	:00							
		:30							

Monday 18/09/2017 To Sunday 24/09/2017

Weather			Daily Training						
			M	T	W	T	F	S	S
	7	:00							
		:30							
	8	:00							
		:15							
		:30							
		:45							
	9	:00							
		:15							
		:30							
		:45							
Running Distance	10	:00							
		:15							
		:30							
		:45							
	11	:00							
		:15							
		:30							
		:45							
	12	:00							
		:15							
		:30							
		:45							
	1	:00							
		:15							
		:30							
		:45							
	2	:00							
		:15							
		:30							
Time		:45							
	3	:00							
		:15							
		:30							
		:45							
	4	:00							
		:15							
		:30							
		:45							
	5	:00							
Comments		:30							
	6	:00							
		:30							
	7	:00							
		:30							
	8	:00							
		:30							

Monday 25/09/2017 To Sunday 01/10/2017

Daily Training

Weather		M	T	W	T	F	S	S
	7 :00							
	:30							
	8 :00							
	:15							
	:30							
	:45							
	9 :00							
	:15							
	:30							
	:45							
Running Distance	10 :00							
	:15							
	:30							
	:45							
	11 :00							
	:15							
	:30							
	:45							
	12 :00							
	:15							
	:30							
	:45							
	1 :00							
	:15							
	:30							
	:45							
	2 :00							
	:15							
	:30							
Time	:45							
	3 :00							
	:15							
	:30							
	:45							
	4 :00							
	:15							
	:30							
	:45							
	5 :00							
Comments	:30							
	6 :00							
	:30							
	7 :00							
	:30							
	8 :00							
	:30							

Monday 02/10/2017 To Sunday 08/10/2017

Weather			Daily Training						
			M	T	W	T	F	S	S
	7	:00							
		:30							
	8	:00							
		:15							
		:30							
		:45							
	9	:00							
		:15							
		:30							
		:45							
Running Distance	10	:00							
		:15							
		:30							
		:45							
	11	:00							
		:15							
		:30							
		:45							
	12	:00							
		:15							
		:30							
		:45							
	1	:00							
		:15							
		:30							
		:45							
	2	:00							
		:15							
		:30							
Time		:45							
	3	:00							
		:15							
		:30							
		:45							
	4	:00							
		:15							
		:30							
		:45							
	5	:00							
Comments		:30							
	6	:00							
		:30							
	7	:00							
		:30							
	8	:00							
		:30							

Monday 09/10/2017 To Sunday 15/10/2017

Weather			Daily Training						
			M	T	W	T	F	S	S
	7	:00							
		:30							
	8	:00							
		:15							
		:30							
		:45							
	9	:00							
		:15							
		:30							
		:45							
Running Distance	10	:00							
		:15							
		:30							
		:45							
	11	:00							
		:15							
		:30							
		:45							
	12	:00							
		:15							
		:30							
		:45							
	1	:00							
		:15							
		:30							
		:45							
	2	:00							
		:15							
		:30							
Time		:45							
	3	:00							
		:15							
		:30							
		:45							
	4	:00							
		:15							
		:30							
		:45							
	5	:00							
Comments		:30							
	6	:00							
		:30							
	7	:00							
		:30							
	8	:00							
		:30							

Monday 16/10/2017 To Sunday 22/10/2017

Weather			Daily Training						
			M	T	W	T	F	S	S
	7	:00							
		:30							
	8	:00							
		:15							
		:30							
		:45							
	9	:00							
		:15							
		:30							
		:45							
	10	:00							
Running Distance		:15							
		:30							
		:45							
	11	:00							
		:15							
		:30							
		:45							
	12	:00							
		:15							
		:30							
		:45							
	1	:00							
		:15							
		:30							
		:45							
	2	:00							
		:15							
		:30							
Time		:45							
	3	:00							
		:15							
		:30							
		:45							
	4	:00							
		:15							
		:30							
		:45							
	5	:00							
Comments		:30							
	6	:00							
		:30							
	7	:00							
		:30							
	8	:00							
		:30							

Monday 23/10/2017 To Sunday 29/10/2017

Weather			Daily Training						
			M	T	W	T	F	S	S
	7	:00							
		:30							
	8	:00							
		:15							
		:30							
		:45							
	9	:00							
		:15							
		:30							
		:45							
	10	:00							
Running Distance		:15							
		:30							
		:45							
	11	:00							
		:15							
		:30							
		:45							
	12	:00							
		:15							
		:30							
		:45							
	1	:00							
		:15							
		:30							
		:45							
	2	:00							
		:15							
		:30							
Time		:45							
	3	:00							
		:15							
		:30							
		:45							
	4	:00							
		:15							
		:30							
		:45							
	5	:00							
Comments		:30							
	6	:00							
		:30							
	7	:00							
		:30							
	8	:00							
		:30							

Monday 30/10/2017 To Sunday 05/11/2017

Weather				M	T	W	T	F	S	S
		7	:00							
			:30							
		8	:00							
			:15							
			:30							
			:45							
		9	:00							
			:15							
			:30							
			:45							
		10	:00							
Running Distance			:15							
			:30							
			:45							
		11	:00							
			:15							
			:30							
			:45							
		12	:00							
			:15							
			:30							
			:45							
		1	:00							
			:15							
			:30							
			:45							
		2	:00							
			:15							
			:30							
Time			:45							
		3	:00							
			:15							
			:30							
			:45							
		4	:00							
			:15							
			:30							
			:45							
		5	:00							
Comments			:30							
		6	:00							
			:30							
		7	:00							
			:30							
		8	:00							
			:30							

Monday 06/11/2017 To Sunday 12/11/2017

Weather			M	T	W	T	F	S	S
	7	:00							
		:30							
	8	:00							
		:15							
		:30							
		:45							
	9	:00							
		:15							
		:30							
		:45							
	10	:00							
Running Distance		:15							
		:30							
		:45							
	11	:00							
		:15							
		:30							
		:45							
	12	:00							
		:15							
		:30							
		:45							
	1	:00							
		:15							
		:30							
		:45							
	2	:00							
		:15							
		:30							
Time		:45							
	3	:00							
		:15							
		:30							
		:45							
	4	:00							
		:15							
		:30							
		:45							
	5	:00							
Comments		:30							
	6	:00							
		:30							
	7	:00							
		:30							
	8	:00							
		:30							

Monday 13/11/2017 To Sunday 19/11/2017

Weather			Daily Training							
			M	T	W	T	F	S	S	
	7	:00								
		:30								
	8	:00								
		:15								
		:30								
		:45								
	9	:00								
		:15								
		:30								
		:45								
Running Distance	10	:00								
		:15								
		:30								
		:45								
	11	:00								
		:15								
		:30								
		:45								
	12	:00								
		:15								
		:30								
		:45								
	1	:00								
		:15								
		:30								
		:45								
	2	:00								
		:15								
		:30								
Time		:45								
	3	:00								
		:15								
		:30								
		:45								
	4	:00								
		:15								
		:30								
		:45								
	5	:00								
Comments		:30								
	6	:00								
		:30								
	7	:00								
		:30								
	8	:00								
		:30								

Daily Training

Weather			M	T	W	T	F	S	S
	7	:00							
		:30							
	8	:00							
		:15							
		:30							
		:45							
	9	:00							
		:15							
		:30							
		:45							
Running Distance	10	:00							
		:15							
		:30							
		:45							
	11	:00							
		:15							
		:30							
		:45							
	12	:00							
		:15							
		:30							
		:45							
	1	:00							
		:15							
		:30							
		:45							
	2	:00							
		:15							
		:30							
Time		:45							
	3	:00							
		:15							
		:30							
		:45							
	4	:00							
		:15							
		:30							
		:45							
	5	:00							
Comments		:30							
	6	:00							
		:30							
	7	:00							
		:30							
	8	:00							
		:30							

Monday 27/11/2017 To Sunday 03/12/2017

Weather			Daily Training						
			M	T	W	T	F	S	S
	7	:00							
		:30							
	8	:00							
		:15							
		:30							
		:45							
	9	:00							
		:15							
		:30							
		:45							
	10	:00							
Running Distance		:15							
		:30							
		:45							
	11	:00							
		:15							
		:30							
		:45							
	12	:00							
		:15							
		:30							
		:45							
	1	:00							
		:15							
		:30							
		:45							
	2	:00							
		:15							
		:30							
Time		:45							
	3	:00							
		:15							
		:30							
		:45							
	4	:00							
		:15							
		:30							
		:45							
	5	:00							
Comments		:30							
	6	:00							
		:30							
	7	:00							
		:30							
	8	:00							
		:30							

Monday 04/12/2017 To Sunday 10/12/2017

Weather			M	T	W	T	F	S	S
	7	:00							
		:30							
	8	:00							
		:15							
		:30							
		:45							
	9	:00							
		:15							
		:30							
		:45							
Running Distance	10	:00							
		:15							
		:30							
		:45							
	11	:00							
		:15							
		:30							
		:45							
	12	:00							
		:15							
		:30							
		:45							
	1	:00							
		:15							
		:30							
		:45							
	2	:00							
		:15							
		:30							
Time		:45							
	3	:00							
		:15							
		:30							
		:45							
	4	:00							
		:15							
		:30							
		:45							
	5	:00							
Comments		:30							
	6	:00							
		:30							
	7	:00							
		:30							
	8	:00							
		:30							

Daily Training

Monday 11/12/2017 To Sunday 17/12/2017

Weather			Daily Training						
			M	T	W	T	F	S	S
	7 :00								
	:30								
	8 :00								
	:15								
	:30								
	:45								
	9 :00								
	:15								
	:30								
	:45								
Running Distance	10 :00								
	:15								
	:30								
	:45								
	11 :00								
	:15								
	:30								
	:45								
	12 :00								
	:15								
	:30								
	:45								
	1 :00								
	:15								
	:30								
	:45								
	2 :00								
	:15								
	:30								
Time	:45								
	3 :00								
	:15								
	:30								
	:45								
	4 :00								
	:15								
	:30								
	:45								
	5 :00								
Comments	:30								
	6 :00								
	:30								
	7 :00								
	:30								
	8 :00								
	:30								

Monday 18/12/2017 To Sunday 24/12/2017

Weather			Daily Training							
			M	T	W	T	F	S	S
	7	:00							
		:30							
	8	:00							
		:15							
		:30							
		:45							
	9	:00							
		:15							
		:30							
		:45							
Running Distance	10	:00							
		:15							
		:30							
		:45							
	11	:00							
		:15							
		:30							
		:45							
	12	:00							
		:15							
		:30							
		:45							
	1	:00							
		:15							
		:30							
		:45							
	2	:00							
		:15							
		:30							
Time		:45							
	3	:00							
		:15							
		:30							
		:45							
	4	:00							
		:15							
		:30							
		:45							
	5	:00							
Comments		:30							
	6	:00							
		:30							
	7	:00							
		:30							
	8	:00							
		:30							

Monday 25/12/2017 To Sunday 31/12/2017

Weather				Daily Training						
			M	T	W	T	F	S	S	
	7	:00								
		:30								
	8	:00								
		:15								
		:30								
		:45								
	9	:00								
		:15								
		:30								
		:45								
Running Distance	10	:00								
		:15								
		:30								
		:45								
	11	:00								
		:15								
		:30								
		:45								
	12	:00								
		:15								
		:30								
		:45								
	1	:00								
		:15								
		:30								
		:45								
	2	:00								
		:15								
		:30								
Time		:45								
	3	:00								
		:15								
		:30								
		:45								
	4	:00								
		:15								
		:30								
		:45								
	5	:00								
Comments		:30								
	6	:00								
		:30								
	7	:00								
		:30								
	8	:00								
		:30								

Run No.	Route	Start	Distance	Time	Avg Speed(Avg Pace)	Calories
e.g. 1	Ingthorpe Ward Running	Wed, 2 Nov 2016 9:45 AM	1.48	16:50:00	11:23	257
1						
2						
3						
4						
5						
6						
7						
8						
9						
10						
11						
12						
13						
14						
15						

Run No.	Route	Start	Distance	Time	Avg Speed(Avg Pace)	Calories
16						
17						
18						
19						
20						
21						
22						
23						
24						
25						
26						
27						
28						
29						
30						

Run No.	Route	Start	Distance	Time	Avg Speed(Avg Pace)	Calories
31						
32						
33						
34						
35						
36						
37						
38						
39						
40						
41						
42						
43						
44						
45						

Run No.	Route	Start	Distance	Time	Avg Speed(Avg Pace)	Calories
46						
47						
48						
49						
50						
51						
52						
53						
54						
55						
56						
57						
58						
59						
60						

Run No.	Route	Start	Distance	Time	Avg Speed(Avg Pace)	Calories
61						
62						
63						
64						
65						
66						
67						
68						
69						
70						
71						
72						
73						
74						
75						

Run No.	Route	Start	Distance	Time	Avg Speed(Avg Pace)	Calories
76						
77						
78						
79						
80						
81						
82						
83						
84						
85						
86						
87						
88						
89						
90						

Run No.	Route	Start	Distance	Time	Avg Speed(Avg Pace)	Calories
91						
92						
93						
94						
95						
96						
97						
98						
99						
100						
101						
102						
103						
104						
105						

Run No.	Route	Start	Distance	Time	Avg Speed(Avg Pace)	Calories
106						
107						
108						
109						
110						
111						
112						
113						
114						
115						
116						
117						
118						
119						
120						

Run No.	Route	Start	Distance	Time	Avg Speed(Avg Pace)	Calories
121						
122						
123						
124						
125						
126						
127						
128						
129						
130						
131						
132						
133						
134						
135						

Run No.	Route	Start	Distance	Time	Avg Speed(Avg Pace)	Calories
136						
137						
138						
139						
140						
141						
142						
143						
144						
145						
146						
147						
148						
149						
150						

Notes

==

Notes

==

Notes

==